15 MIN

15 Minutes with Mom
Thoughts and Memories from a Woman Born Already Grown

by Rick Kemp

15 Minutes with Mom

15 Minutes with Mom

15 MINUTES WITH MOM

Copyright © 2017 by Rick Kemp

Published by Constant Reader Press

No part of this work may be reproduced without express written permission of the publisher except brief quotations for review purposes.

This is an memoir- and interview-based, nonfiction work expressing the thoughts and beliefs of the author. The views and ideas expressed here are solely those of the author and the subject..

Cover Design by
Constant Reader Press
© 2017

ISBN-13:978-1979776035

ISBN-10:1979776032

15 Minutes with Mom

For Especially Mom

and her children --
Ed, Linda, Bob, Brenda, and Fred --
and their children --
and their children's children --
and their children's children children --
and for all who have come into the family
for it is all of us for whom Mom lives and
breathes

15 Minutes with Mom

List of Thoughts

List of Thoughts	6
Introduction	8
On Scary Stories, Eddie's Diapers, and Moving to Maryland	13
On Memories, Cemeteries, and Siblings	17
On Hot Houses, Staying with Linda, and Being Born Grown	21
On Food, the Depression, and Discipline	25
On the Big House, Mama, and Meeting "Your Daddy"	29
On Sinuses, Smoking, and Jim Trader	34
On Play, Blackberry Wine, and Soot	37
On Wedding, Quicks, and Missing Cake	43
On Glasses, Brenda, and Bobby	51
On Moving, The Big House, and Moving Again	57
On Vitamins, Yeast, and Forced Fish	60
On Insurance, Cancer, and Co-Pays	77
On Maggie the Dog, Brenda and Joe's Trick, and Fred's Return	82
On Six Weeks with Ricky, Jelly Beans, and Kaka	92

15 Minutes with Mom

On Rain, Getting Sick, and Pipe Smoking   99

On Steak, Honey Bee, and Friendly's   101

Introduction

For a brief moment in my life I had the fortunate opportunity to talk to my then 88- (now 89- as I complete this book) year-old mother at least twice a day for about 15 minutes at a time. It didn't dawn on me for weeks to write down what we'd said, but eventually I wised up and wrote down after she and I would hang up all that I could about her life.

In this short book are 20 of those conversations -- some brief, some longer. I left out the pleasantries and mundaneness where we discussed the weather or what we had for breakfast, choosing instead to coax out of Mom tidbits, stories, vignettes, and moments of her life. Too often we wait till we *can't* know the stories of the people we love, enjoy, and cherish. Though brief, my intention was to give us all moments of Juanita Frances Kemp that we might not otherwise have known.

On a personal note, I am so very thankful that I had this opportunity to learn so much more about Mom. At first, as you will see, the memories she had were full of cobwebs and crust and rust, but as the engine of her mind oiled up the moments flowed better and stronger. I don't know if it's the place of a child to feel pride for his parent for it always seems to be that the parent feels pride for her child. Notwithstanding that I am so proud of Mom. Though the stories aren't long and the book is but brief, one clear topic that doesn't waver, never pauses, never backs up is Mom's unending love for her children. I am proud of my Mom, and honored to have had this opportunity, and thankful that I still have her here to speak with her and expand on these stories. Take the time to do the same -- call her, speak with her, ask her. She might hesitate at first, but that comes from a lifetime of pointing her vision and worldview outward toward especially her children and grandchildren, but also to most people as she was born "fully grown." It's nice to get her to turn that vision around and ask her to see inside of herself. The memories are sometimes gray and cloudy, but help her add some light and there is still great moments to reveal.

    Please remember that these conversations were originally private moments between son and mother and that Mom is 88 years old. Things might not always flow the way we expect as I've tried to keep her language, syntax, and vocabulary the way she said it. There might also be moments that surprise you, perhaps even shock you, but take this all as the way it's intended -- to know about Frances what we might not otherwise know. I'm sorry if you are not mentioned in the conversations -- the stories went where they went and largely focused on her life in Bennettsville, South Carolina, and Baltimore, Maryland from about as early as 1928. I'm sorry if anything offends -- it certainly isn't my or Mom's intentions.

    I hope you enjoy the book and find it meaningful, insightful, and inspirational.

    Mom, with all my heart.

15 Minutes with Mom

November 2017   -- Rick

On Scary Stories, Eddie's Diapers, and Moving to Maryland

Me: Aunt Irene used to tell the scariest ghost stories.

Mom: Yeah, she was really good at them. She had quite a memory before she got sick. And she really loved to tell stories.

Me: I remember on that trip we took cross country that she told us a story about a heart thrown into a fire that kept beating.

Mom: Yeah. I don't know.

Me: And you all -- you, Aunt Irene, grandma -- always used to talk about some white dog.

Mom: Yeah, we had a white dog.

Me: But this one was some story about a dog that came in and sat at the foot of someone's bed and said, "You're going to die." Of course, how did anyone know if the person died?

Mom: Well, I don't have no idea about that. It was my grandma Quick, my daddy's mama, that could really tell a story. She'd come and visit us and sit in a rocker and we'd sit on the floor and listen. Course, there wasn't no TV then. We didn't even have a radio at that time.

Me: She'd visit at your house?

Mom: Yeah. Daddy's place on the farm. At that time there weren't no Pampers or stuff like that so you had to use cloth diapers so she'd sit and dry Eddie's diapers and tell us stories.

Me: How old were you?

Mom: About 10.

Me: But you said she'd dry Eddie's diapers. He's your oldest child. How could you have been 10?

Mom: Oh. I mean when I was 10 and later after Eddie was born, too. She sure loved Eddie. Her first great-grandchild and all. She sure could tell a story.

Me: So you, Linda, Eddie, and Dad lived there?

Mom: No. No. After Linda was born, Matt was likely up in Maryland. He'd come up for two or three months at a time. When he came back down he packed us all up and went to Maryland. He said he'd checked

15 Minutes with Mom

with the law and could take the kids from me if I didn't go. I'd never seen no law before, so I didn't know no better. I packed up and went. Everyone else followed after.

<u>Me</u>: OK, Mom. That's our time. Love you.

<u>Mom</u>: Love you more.

<u>Me</u>: Remember, when I call back I'd like to hear about the earliest memory you have.

"LOVE YOU MORE"

On Memories, Cemeteries, and Siblings

Me: So you've got a story to tell me?

Mom: Well, the first thing I remember, well, I was born July 8 and Irene was born August 31, and I'm two years older than she is so I don't remember her being born. I think I remember LT being born and me having to take care of him somewhat. But I am nine years older than Ann and I really remember taking care of her. See, we had to work in the field when we were five years old.

Me: So how much older than LT are you?

Mom: Hmm. Well, how old is LT? I can't remember. I'll have to ask Ann. There was another baby. A little sister, born between LT and Ann. She didn't live but an hour and then she died. Sad. Sad. Then there was another after Ann who, well, it was born dead. Uncle Johnny, Eleanor's grandfather, made a little wood coffin and lined it in white linen.

Me: Where did they bury her?

Mom: Not far from where we lived. You know, they built homes over that cemetery.

Me: Were there tombstones?

Mom: No. I don't think there were any. I thought it was illegal to build over a cemetery.

Me: Well, they might not have known. Without tombstones after a while there's not much left.

Mom: My uncle was buried there, too. Well, I have no idea.

Me: So that's your earliest memory?

Mom: Right now it is. Check back with me tomorrow and it might be another story. (She laughs).

Me: (Laughing). All right, Mom. I love you.

Mom: Love you more. Bye.

"I Really Remember Taking Care of Her"

15 Minutes with Mom

On Hot Houses, Staying with Linda, and Being Born Grown

Me: It's supposed to be hot today.

Mom: Over one hundred. You know growing up we didn't have a fan. Remember that little house over from the high school?

Me: Yes, ma'am.

Mom: It had a concrete floor. It was so hot one summer Linda had you, me, and Freddy stay with her because she had air conditioning. During Vietnam, Brenda stayed with Ann and Eddie. Linda didn't have room for all of us. So hot in that little house that the candles melted on the table. Then Daddy bought me a fan. First I'd ever had.

<u>Me</u>:   What else have you been thinking about?

<u>Mom</u>: The strongest memories I have is taking care of Ann after she was born. There was a wood stove and a pump and we had to pump water. And Daddy and them would go off to the woods and chop wood for the fireplace and stove.

<u>Me</u>:   Was it a round stove?

<u>Mom</u>: It was a cast iron stove. No, not always round, sometimes. It was square and the griddles were hot and heavy you had to be careful. In the kitchen we had a long table and on one side was a bench and the

other had two chairs and the end had a chair. That's where we ate. We had an icebox to keep our food cold. You had to have a big chunk of ice in it.

Me: Where did you get the ice?

Mom: I don't know, but it was a big chunk. You bought it from some place. It was a hard life how we were raised, but we didn't really know it. We thought everyone lived that way. We worked in the field by the time we were five, but I was with mama most of the time. We didn't have play time. It was like I was born already grown.

"I WAS BORN ALREADY GROWN."

15 Minutes with Mom

On Food, the Depression, and Discipline

Mom: So Jennifer done fixed my hair. She brought me some chicken dish like an eclair but with chicken.

Me: An eclair? An empanada you mean?

Mom: Yeah... I don't know. It was good. So mama had a pantry and we all helped her can. We had tomatoes, okra, corn, tomato soup, peaches, blueberries, huckleberries...

Me: What's a huckleberry?

15 Minutes with Mom

Mom: Well, blackberries are big and grow on vines, blueberries are small and grow on trees. Huckleberries are between them.

Me: What color are they?

Mom: Black, too. We'd dig the potatoes, strike off the top. Sweet potatoes. Daddy made a sweet potato hill like a teepee with straw inside and all around and dirt on top to keep the sweet potatoes all winter. We had a lot. We never went hungry. We had hogs and chickens. Eggs. We'd slaughter the hogs and put up hams and shoulders in the smokehouse. You know the difference between a ham and a shoulder?

Me: No. Not really.

Mom: We'd make sausage, blood sausage, liver pudding, clean the intestines and fry them -- called chittlings. You talk about a bad smell. Woo-eee. We'd eat everything off a hog but what was inside the intestines.

Me: So you were born in 1928.

Mom: 1928.

Me: That's a year before the Great Depression started. What do you remember about the Great Depression?

Mom: We'd get only one pair of shoes to last a year. And Daddy was afraid to let us go outside to play or to go do anything but work because we couldn't afford a doctor bill if anything happened. Mama would use old remedies. It was hard to afford five pairs of shoes for five youngins. Kids today don't know, don't get it. You, either.

Me: I know, Mom.

Mom: It was hard. Daddy was strict and harsh. He did what he had to do I guess. I guess it was the same with my children. I had to do what I had to do to get by sometimes. We'd pick cotton when we were five years old. Then after we ate supper, we called it "supper" then not dinner, we'd clean up and shuck peas and beans for mama to cook the next day. I had rickets. You know what rickets are?

<u>Me</u>:   Not really.

<u>Mom</u>: My legs were so big and sores on my rear were broken open. I had to sit on a pillow cause I wouldn't eat well. Ate molasses and bread and fat back and worked in the fields.

"I HAD TO DO WHAT I HAD TO DO TO GET BY SOMETIMES"

On the Big House, Mama, and Meeting "Your Daddy"

Mom: We lived on a farm you know. No electricity, no running water. Kerosene lamps lit the place. After years we moved to the Big House. We thought we were living high. Electricity, running water. We even had a bathroom. Plenty to eat. We had the most beautiful garden. Planted watermelons, and Daddy knew exactly when to pick them and you'd better not touch nerry one till he said so. I don't remember carrots, but we had beans, peas, okra, tomato, squash. We had zucchini. People would say, "Mr. Quick's family is the busiest around." You know how people have green lawns now? Daddy didn't want to see any grass in the lawn. If there was, you had to pull it. We raked and swept that lawn.

<u>Me</u>: What about play? What do you remember?

<u>Mom</u>: I never played. Sunday we'd walk a long way to church. Saturday they'd go out to play sometimes if the work was done, but I'd stay with Mama. Always hung around Mama. Me and Mama had a very good relationship up till she got dementia. Then it was hard. She didn't like how I had to take care of her. One time I was washing her in the tub and I pushed on her chest so she'd lean back. She balled up her fist as if to

punch me and said, "You're as mean as Ann used to be." I told her, "You hurt my feelings" and she said she was sorry.

    The day she died I had to withdraw all the money she had to pay for the place she was in. I said to her I'd be back and she said, "You better be back." It took every dime she had. I'm so glad I'd paid for everything [the funeral] beforehand. I'd pay a little at a time till it was all paid for. Fred wrote me a card to say how wonderful it was that I'd done that. The family only had to pay for flowers and the place to eat afterward. I knew I had to do it. I didn't have the money to pay everything. All Fred had to do was pick up the phone and call the undertaker and that was it. Then I started putting away money to help pay for her house till Fred took it over. Bob lived there, and oh my what a mess it was.

Me: Yeah, it was. It's sad.
Mom: I saw your daddy in town. I don't know why he was hanging out in Bennettsville. I saw him on a bench by the courthouse. You know people went to the movies and milled around. I guess I was in town because I was working. I made camouflage netting for the war. You know?

Me: Yes, ma'am.

Mom: I met him in December and married him in January.

"MR. QUICK'S FAMILY IS THE BUSIEST AROUND"

On Sinuses, Smoking, and Jim Trader

<u>Me</u>: I'm doing okay. My cold turned into a sinus infection.

<u>Mom</u>: I never had sinus trouble till I married Jim Trader. He smoked like a fiend. I'd stay in my bedroom when he and one of his friends would talk and drink in the living room usually all day on a Saturday or Sunday. I'd open the door and it was like the house was on fire the whole hallway filled with smoke. I had to make him go outside to smoke. I couldn't stand it no

more. Every since then I've had sinus problems.

"I Couldn't stand it no more"

15 Minutes with Mom

15 Minutes with Mom

On Play, Blackberry Wine, and Soot

Me: So you've told me a lot about how hard it was. Tell me about when you played.

Mom: I was born on old woman. I didn't play. LT and Irene were the playenest children I ever seen and then when Ann got big enough, her, too. They'd put on shows for some colored people who lived near us and they'd just loved those shows. They'd play ball with a rock. They'd use a rim off an old car as a steering wheel - that was their car.

Me: But you didn't play?

Mom: Well, I'm telling you the truth --- I worked with Mama.

Me: OK. Tell me about working with Grandma.

Mom: We had a bottle of blackberry wine. There were three tin tubs on a bench. We'd boil the clothes then put them in the first tub to wash, and the other tubs were for rinsing. Scrub and rinse, scrub and rinse. And we'd drink some blackberry wine [she laughs].

Me: [Laughing]. Mom--I thought you never drank.

Mom: Just blackberry wine [she laughs hard]. Daddy didn't know. I don't think he did. We had a scrub board. When we came up [to Baltimore] we got a place by the B&O Railroad Station. We had one bed for your father, Eddie, Linda, and me. We'd sleep feet to head, feet to head all on one bed. Ed and Linda would sit on the bed when I got their bath ready. I had to carry them or they'd be covered in soot. I'd wash the clothes in the bathtub with a washboard. We were on the third floor and Eddie and me would walk down three flights to hang the clothes. Poor little guy tried to help so much. Poor baby Linda I had to leave sitting on the floor. When I came back she'd be covered in soot again and I'd have to wash her over.

Me: How old were Linda and Eddie?

Mom: Eddie was eighteen months and Linda was four months. Your daddy would move us all the time.

Me. Why?

Mom: I have no idea. I felt like I was always cleaning dirty apartments. Back then you didn't pay a security deposit. People just moved and left it filthy. It was hard. I would get a job making .75 cents per hour. Best I ever did was $1.25 per hour. Hard life, but I'm thankful for my children. They're all I ever wanted. I'd do anything for them if I could. I only went to school two months out of the year. January and February when it was too cold to do any farming. Nothing else to do.

<u>Me</u>: Was it a one-room school house?

<u>Mom</u>: Sure was. And we walked to it, too.

<u>Me</u>: How far?

<u>Mom</u>: From about Linda's house to Eddie's house distance. Two to two-and-a-half miles each way. I'll never forget. [she chuckles]. One time a man stopped to ask if we wanted a ride. Me and Lawrence and Irene. I guess LT was too young to go to

school yet. One of those cars with a thing in the back that came up.

<u>Me</u>: A jump seat?

<u>Mom</u>: Yeah. I guess. Well, we three got ourselves in there [chuckles] and when he put it in gear the car jerked and took off. Irene fell over the back of the car and into the road. Lawrence started yelling, "My sister done fell out!" [she laughs hard]. We had some good laughs.

"I'M THANKFUL FOR MY CHILDREN"

15 Minutes with Mom

On Wedding, Quicks, and Missing Cake

Me: So tell me about your wedding.

Mom: We got married at the justice of the peace at the courthouse in Bennettsville. Irene and LT were there. There's a lot of Quicks down there. One of them passed us in the courthouse and said to your daddy, "There's lots of us Quicks down here. You better be good to her."

Me: Grandma and Grandpa didn't show up?

Mom: No. I don't know how we got there.

15 Minutes with Mom

Me: Why didn't the come?

Mom: I don't know. They didn't go to anyone's wedding.

Me: What did you wear?

Mom: I don't remember.

Me: How old were you?

Mom: Eighteen in July. I got married in January.

Me: Eighteen and a half?

Mom: Yup. Eighteen and a half.

Me: So Aunt Irene was sixteen and LT was fourteen? That's who went to your wedding? I'm surprised.

Mom: I didn't even get a cake.

Me: I guess we've made up for that cake over these years.

Mom: Sure did.

"You Better Be Good To Her"

15 Minutes with Mom

On Pushing the Baby Buggy, Coming to Maryland, and Matt Rambling

<u>Mom</u>: We weren't married long, I was pregnant, when he went off back to Baltimore. Then he came back. He was always going and coming back, going and coming back. He didn't know anything about farming more than the man in the moon. But he was going to do some planting. So he moved us into this old country house way out in the country. He

didn't know how to farm. One day we were out in the field chopping cotton. I'd left poor little Eddie playing on the floor while I was out there. See, the cotton grew right up next to the house. Matt got mad and stormed off toward the house. John, a cousin, and Irene were helping us. When I saw him go we all figured if he wasn't going to be out there chopping cotton then were weren't either. So we went off to the house, too. By the time we got there he had done left. So, I had one of those old baby buggies -- you know what I mean?

Me: Yes, ma'am.

Mom: Well, I put Eddie in the buggy and packed what I could on top of him and went on up the dirt road toward Mama's.

Me: How far was it?

Mom: I don't know. It was a good long piece. He'd go back to Baltimore at the drop of a hat. He came back and I got pregnant with Linda and he took off back to Baltimore. When it came time to give birth to Linda he came back. We went to the hospital.

Me: Oh, Linda wasn't born on the farm?

Mom: Yes. She was born on the farm.

Me: What about the hospital?

Mom: She was born in the hospital. Both of them were born in the hospital.

Me: Oh, I see, while living on a farm.

Mom: We went on Saturday and she was born on Sunday. He liked Gladis and stayed with her rather than with us, see? When Linda was born he left again for Baltimore. He stayed four months and then came back saying he had a place for us and that's when he told me the lawyer said he could take the children if I didn't go with him. So dummy me, I didn't know nothin about no law, went with him. That was when we lived in that third floor apartment across from the train depot off Lombard Street.

Daddy came up after about a month and asked Matt if we could go back with him for awhile. Daddy was crazy about Ed and Linda. Matt said, "Yes," so Daddy took us and the Greyhound back down. Matt's own mother said he should have never gotten married. He was always a rambler. Could never be still. He wouldn't ever stay put when he was young. Went in the Navy and that made him still for awhile. He couldn't keep a job. Get a good paying job and then leave it. If it weren't for the rambling he was a good man.

Me: How many times did you go back and forth to Bennettsville?

Mom: Oh, it was mainly your father who did the rambling. I went as often as I could to see my family. Then they started moving up here to Maryland. Little by little, one after the other.

"HE DIDN'T KNOW ANYTHING ABOUT FARMING MORE THAN THE MAN IN THE MOON"

On Glasses, Brenda, and Bobby

<u>Mom</u>: Well, I spoke with Brenda and she said she was taking some medicine because her teeth hurt her so much. When she was 18 months old she was vomiting and vomiting so much that I said I wasn't going to give her anything else to eat or drink till the doctor came. I was so dumb. Of course she needed something to drink but I didn't give it to her. She had to go to the hospital and that's when we found out she needed glasses. Tiny lenses the size of nickles. And she loved Romper Room with that lady who came on. She'd sit down and watch it

with a snack. But she'd try to flush her glasses down the toilet. That's till she found out she could watch Romper Room better with her glasses on and then took them and stopped trying to flush them. She was five. I should have sent her to kindergarten. She'd sit on the front step and watch all the kids go to school. I was pregnant with Freddy at the time.

    She was sitting between the steps of our house and the one next door. I thought she was just watching. I went to the window to see where she was but I didn't see her. Next thing I know I hear her screaming. I was pregnant with Fred. I rushed out here. I'd dressed her in a little corduroy pants. Shoes and socks. I don't recall what shirt she had on. She was stomping her feet. Her pants were on fire. There was a fireman

right across the street but he didn't budge.
A man come running down the street to
help. He took off his coat . . . no, wait, he
told me to go inside and get something to
put out the fire, so I ran in and grabbed a
coat. He threw it over her and patted out the
fire Then he put us in his car and took us to
Bon Secour Hospital. They asked if we had
insurance, but we didn't. Her leg was black.
So they put liniment oil on it and wrapped it
up in bandages. My poor baby was
screaming and peeing, poor thing, and
calling to me. They said they'd need to keep
her and asked what insurance we had but we
didn't have any so they said bring her back
on Friday. When Friday came, Matt
wheeled her in a stroller back to Bon
Secour. It took forever to get those
bandages off and her screaming and crying.

15 Minutes with Mom

Mama and Mary Lee [sister-in-law] would wheel Brenda up there in the stroller to go to the clinic to get treated. My mama was such a good person Then next thing I know, see, you used to get your groceries in paper bags and I folded them and I found her setting them on fire. I told her, "Brenda, you're going to set yourself on fire again and you're putting everyone in danger. Yourself, your brothers and sister, your whole family." So she started crying. I'd set her in her stroller and put her before the window so she could see the people go by. I had to keep an eye on her all the time.
<u>Me</u>:   Why no school?
<u>Mom</u>: I have no idea. She loved to see the flames. I told her since she might burn us all up that if she kept doing it I'd have to

15 Minutes with Mom

send her away where she could be watched all the time. So she stopped. Poor girl.

Me: She's such a great spirit.

Mom: Such a wonderful personal You always worry about your kids. From the time they're born till after they're dead. I think of Bobby all the time. He was such a good man but terrible to himself. His problems started when he went to work for Eddie Elmore downtown at those massage parlors. Then he got into drugs. I worried about him all the time.

"YOU ALWAYS WORRY ABOUT YOUR KIDS"

15 Minutes with Mom

On Moving, The Big House, and Moving Again

Me: So, Mom, I wanted to hear about where you lived in the South.

Mom: Not tonight. I've got company.

Me: OK. Well, think about it and we'll talk tomorrow.

Mom: It was Matt who moved us all the time up here. We moved so often. Down south we only moved three times. There was the one bedroom house where Mama and Daddy lived when they got married. Lawrence and I were born there. Then the three bedroom house. Then the Big House. We thought we were living high on the hog there. Boys slept in one room, girls in another, and Mama and Daddy in the other.

Me: What was the kitchen like?

Mom: Sometimes big kitchens and little baths or you'd get big baths and little kitchens.

Me: Why did my father move so often?

Mom: No idea.

Me: Was it money?

Mom: Maybe. One place we only paid $12 per week. They didn't have security deposits then. So people left the places anyway they wanted. It seems he'd move us then take off back to Bennettsville.

Me: Was the three bedroom house the one you showed me?* It was made of cinder blocks.

15 Minutes with Mom

Mom: No. That was Lawrence's place. Ours was up on the hill from there.

*When I lived in Florida, Mom visited me for six weeks. While driving back to Maryland we stopped in Bennettsville so she could show me around and so I could do research for a book.

"NOT TONIGHT. I'VE GOT COMPANY."

15 Minutes with Mom

On Vitamins, Yeast, and Forced Fish

Mom: You know what rickets are?

Me: Not really.

Mom: I had a vitamin deficiency. All I'd eat was fat back, molasses, and bread. Then when Mama had Irene I'd sit right next to the bed on a little chair. I was only 2. My mama's mama, my grandmother, came to help take care and feed me. In those days a woman had to stay in bed for nine days after giving birth. They said my butt was so poor I had to sit on a pillow and my legs were so swollen that they looked like they'd burst if you touched them. I loved chicken. In those days we didn't fry chicken. We baked or boiled it but didn't fry it. I got down from that little chair and went out to the kitchen and climbed up the safe and pulled down the chicken and ate some.

Me: Is a safe like a refrigerator?

Mom: No. Like a china cabinet where you kept food. Grandma had cooked chicken and put it in there and I got me some. Mama was so happy that I ate something different that she cried. You know what palegin is?*

Me: No. What is it?

Mom: I had that, too. It's a vitamin deficiency. My hands and back of my legs were scaly like a fish. I had to drink yeast. We couldn't afford the pills so we got a powder and you mixed it in a glass and stirred it up. Daddy watched over me twice a day while I drank it to make sure I got it all down. It was awful stuff.

Me: Yeast? Like to make bread?

Mom: Yes. Yeast. Y . . . e . . . a . . . s . . . t. Yeast. It's a wonder I've survived. God has watched over me all these years. Mama would cook big pots of greens, turnips, salads, beans, peas, cabbage all the time. But I wouldn't eat it.

Me: All you ever ate was bread, molasses, and fat back?

Mom: No. When I met Matt I started eating everything. I guess I ate some other stuff. Mama would fry okra and I'd eat it. I loved gravy . . . still do. Over chicken or over steak.

Me: So you had plenty of chickens to slaughter.

15 Minutes with Mom

Mom: Oh, plenty of chicken. We never wanted for chicken or eggs. We had plenty of that.

Me: What about steak? Did you kill a cow?

Mom: Mama would buy that at the market when she could once in awhile. Lard was rationed during the Depression. Times were tough. You know lard -- to cook with? She'd go to the store to buy lard and would have to buy fish to get the lard.

Me: Huh? I don't understand that.

Mom: To get the lard she had to buy fish.

Me: Why?

Mom: I have no idea. The man would make her buy some fish to buy the lard. I guess he had too much fish. [she laughs]

Me: Oh, I see. He held the lard hostage and made her buy the fish to get it.

15 MINUTES WITH MOM

Mom: Yeah, I suppose.

*pellagra is a vitamin deficiency that can cause diarrhea, dermatitis, and dementia.

"I GUESS HE HAD TOO MUCH FISH"

On Flu Shots, Learning Lessons, and the Mysterious Shot

Mom: I just came back from downstairs.
Me: Getting your flu shot?
Mom: Yes. They say it'll ache for a day or two and to move my arm around to keep it from getting stiff. Some of them got two shots -- flu and shingles, but I didn't know you had to order the shingles shot in advance. I'll just have to get it next year. Ann can't get a shot here -- her insurance

won't pay for it, but I tell her she needs to get a shot. She says she ain't worried about it. I don't know why I bother. I've always been that way -- I shouldn't stick my nose in other people's business. I'm 88 -- if I haven't learned by now I guess I'll never learn.

Me: That's true.

Mom: One shot we got about knocked us out. We were layed out on the front porch sweating and laughing and moaning. I don't know what it was.

Me: Maybe a polio shot?

Mom: Maybe. I don't know. But it was powerful.

Me: How old were you?

Mom: Seven or eight. But Ann was born and she got it worst of all, so I must have been about ten.

15 Minutes with Mom

"I shouldn't stick my nose in other people's business"

On American Pickers, Philosophy of the Modern World, and Running after Children

Me: I saw this coffee grinder on TV on *American Pickers*. You know that show?

Mom: No. But we had a coffee grinder. Ground up the beans.

Me: Right.

Mom: I saw on Facebook where there was a picture of a sifter -- you know -- for flour.

And it asked if you knew what it was, so I pushed "Like." Of course I knew what it was.

Me: Yeah, I saw that one, too.

Mom: Then there was another one with a toilet.

Me: A toilet or an outhouse?

Mom: Outhouse. We had all different kinds and sizes. Alex [Volberding] asked Linda why I was "liking" all these things and Linda said, "Because she used to use all that stuff." I'll never forget I took Freddie to South Carolina one time. He had to go to the bathroom so I sent him outside. When he came back he said, "It won't flush." [we both laugh hard]. The world is so crazy now.

Me: Well, it's really no more crazy than before. It's just that we know more about everything today because the news is always running.

Mom: No it ain't. It's far worse today.

Me: Well, look at it like this. When Grandma lost the twins at birth did you all call the police?

Mom: Of course not. They died while being born -- that happened all the time.

Me: But today you'd have to call the police, right?

Mom: I'm not sure about that.

Me: I'm pretty sure you would. So that shows a big difference over time.

Mom: I don't know. We never had a car on the farm. Daddy had one at some point but it didn't work. So strange up here with cars running right in front of your door. I didn't want my children killed, so Eddie and Linda had to sit on the stoop and not move. One day the landlord was sitting in chairs on the sidewalk talking with other guys and he asked if Eddie could come down off the stoop. I let him, but I watched him from the window every moment. I'd fly out that door if someone tried to hurt my kids. Like you. I was ironing and the gate was latched, but you unlatched it and went down the alley toward Frederick Road when we lived on Loudon Avenue. I saw all the way down the road that some lady had picked you up. I went flying down there the whole way screaming, "That's my baby! That's my baby!" till I got to you. See how fast a child can disappear? And Bobby, that boy. Daddy put chicken wire all around the porch to keep Bobby in, but that didn't stop him. He climbed right over it, then tossed his tricycle over the fence, then climbed the fence and went riding off. I about lost my mind when Eddie went to Vietnam. I didn't know anything about war. I didn't know if I'd ever see him again. All those poor boys who didn't come home. Such a shame.

Me: But he came home.

Mom: He sure did. And he got married. He lived up in Connecticut.

Me: I thought it was Massachusetts.

Mom: Maybe it was. I'll have to ask. He worked at a High's store.

Me: Didn't he live above a High's store in Glen Burnie.

Mom: I think so. You remember that? You were very young.

Me: Yes, ma'am.

15 Minutes with Mom

"I'D FLY OUT THAT DOOR IF SOMEONE TRIED TO HURT MY KIDS"

On Bicycles, Skates, and Bowling

Me: You know you haven't mailed me anything.

Mom: Well, I mailed you a picture and it came back.

Me: It's like riding a bike -- if you get tossed off you have to get back on.

Mom: I tried riding a bike once. It threw me over the handlebar and I got a bloody nose. I said, "Forget you" and never got back on another one except the kind that stands still. I can't skate neither.

Me: I have no balance. I can ride a bike but not skate.

15 Minutes with Mom

Mom: I signed up to bowl. Me, Irene, Geraldine, and another girl. They about laughed us out of that place. They'd gather to watch how bad we were. I'd keep throwing the ball in the gutter. Next time around, though, we came in 2nd place.

Me: You know it was bowling that made me start to dislike sports. I'd throw the ball and it would go in the gutter. You and Aunt Irene would get so mad at me. I was just a little kid . . .

Mom: Yeah, well . . . .

"Forget You"

On Insurance, Cancer, and Co-Pays

<u>Me</u>: So we got the insurance worked out for the boys.

<u>Mom</u>: I'm so glad. We were on social services when you were a child. You had those seizures and when the surgeon said he'd found a knot in your brain that was causing them he said you'd likely grow out of it, but then he said he couldn't see us anymore because the state didn't pay him enough.

<u>Me</u>: Can you believe doctors say that? It's crazy.

15 Minutes with Mom

Mom: When Daddy was sick and I was helping Mama take care of him I had a doctor appointment and I wasn't going to go because Mama needed help with Daddy. She said he was sleeping well and that I should go, so I did. I'd been seeing one doctor but he stopped seeing me because he wasn't paid enough, so I went to Dr. Chung. He examined me and said I'd need a DNC and a hysterectomy right away. That was on a Friday and I think the surgery was on Monday or Tuesday. It was cancer.

Me: That's the cancer? I've never known that. I thought you had thyroid cancer.

Mom: No. I had to have part of my thyroid taken out. I have part of it and it's swollen. Causes me to not lose weight. When I was pregnant with Bobby I had to take two buses to get to Lutheran Hospital to have a breathing test done to see if I could give birth to him. Of course I did.

Me: Do you mean that they were considering a C-section? Or were they going to have to abort?

Mom: I think C-section. Either way I passed the test and gave birth to Bobby. I had six children all full term and never had a problem. You were my last and the easiest to carry. I felt good and was in good shape. Then afterward I hemorrhaged a lot. The nurse fixed me up and packed me, but when I went home I kept hemorrhaging. It went on and on. Of course I couldn't have anymore children after that.

Me: I guess I broke the mold.

Mom: [Laughing]. Yeah, that's so. Now today I have the best insurance. I got insurance when I turned sixty-five and then when I was seventy-two Linda helped me get AARP insurance to fill the gap. Except for my monthly payment and co-pay I haven't had to pay another cent in all these years. I have to pay the co-pay for prescriptions, but it's not much. Much better than what a lot of people have to pay. I pay $175 every month, but it's worth it.

"I HAD SIX CHILDREN ALL FULL TERM AND NEVER HAD A PROBLEM"

15 Minutes with Mom

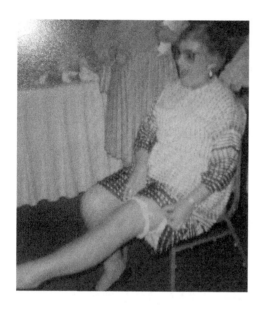

On Maggie the Dog, Brenda and Joe's Trick, and Fred's Return

Mom: I don't know why that dog has to bark at every little thing.

Me: Well why did you get a dog that barks so much?

Mom: I didn't get her. I was sitting at my table when Brenda and Joe came to the door carrying a little dog. Joe got it from his work for Brenda, but their landlord wouldn't let them keep it. So she comes to the door with this cutest little puppy and I fawned all over it and I said I wished I could keep it and Brenda spoke up and said, "She's your's. We brought her for you."

Me: So they set you up? [We laugh]

Mom: Yup, I guess so. I wasn't supposed to have her neither but she didn't bark then. So I'd keep her in my room and when I had to take her somewhere I'd wrap her up till we got to the car. But I couldn't pay for the doctor bills and shots and her nails and hair so Fred said he'd take her. But when he and Sheri broke up there wasn't anyone to watch her when he had to go on his long trips, so I took her back and Fred paid the bills for her.

Me: That was nice of him.

Mom: Sure was. But now she barks at every little thing. I can have her here -- it's ok. But I've got to shoo her away from the door whenever anyone comes in because I can't hear what people are saying when she's yapping.

Me: I know. I can't hear you over the phone when she does that. Tell Maggie she and I are going to have to for a few rounds when I get home.

Mom: [laughs]

"I FAWNED ALL OVER IT AND I SAID I WISHED I COULD KEEP IT"

15 Minutes with Mom

On Not Travelling, Smearing Cakes, and Walking out Drunk

<u>Me</u>: I was wondering if you ever went anywhere besides Bennettsville and Maryland when you lived on the farm?

<u>Mom</u>: No. Myrtle Beach was close to where we lived but we never even went there. We didn't have a car. Well, Daddy eventually bought an old car but we didn't really go anywhere in it. We were poor. I don't know nothing about South Carolina except where I was born.

<u>Me</u>: Well what happened with the car?

15 Minutes with Mom

Mom: I have no idea. I suppose it broke down.

Me: I mean what was it's purpose?

Mom: If there was no work on Saturday some of 'em would go to town t=and see a movie. It was only .10 or .15 cents back then. I worked. I tied camouflage netting for the soldiers. I worked in a cotton mill. I'd stay with Aunt Sarah and Uncle Bryant when I worked the cotton mill or with Aunt Fanny when I was at the camouflage factory. All the places in South Carolina and I'm like a stranger to them. I didn't go no place till we got up here and Eddie Elmore started taking us places. And then you and Jessica took me places. Last time I went someplace was Washington, D.C. when you and the boys and Tabitha took me. Remember?

Me: Yes, ma'am.

Mom: We worked at night, me and Margery. When we got back to her house we'd have to do the laundry and other chores then we'd sleep and get up and go back to work at the factory at night. I made $5.00. I'd buy material, different colors, for Mama to make dresses for her, Irene, Ann, and me. I had to pay $2.50 to stay with my aunts and uncles in town.

Me: So it was $5.00 per week? Wow!

Mom: Yeah. $5.00 per week. I wasn't any good at the cotton mill but I was pretty good at the camouflage factory tying bits of materials. Then I worked at a tomato factory. Hot tomatoes would come down the line and you had to grab them, peel them, and take out the core. You got paid by the basket full. At Brendon Bakery the cakes would come down a conveyor belt and

I took my hand and covered the cake in icing. And jelly rolls. Know them? I'd take the imitation jelly and spread it all over.

Me: With your bare hands?

Mom: Yup. [she laughs]. Then I Worked at Paul Jones Distillery. I'd come out swaying never having taken a drink. [laughs]. It was down south of Baltimore.

Me: I think it was by the airport.

Mom: I don't know. Then there was the peanut factory. The peanuts would come down the conveyor belt and I'd have to take off the faulty ones.

Me: How could you tell if they were salty?

Mom: [laughs]. Faulty. F. . . A . . . U . . . L . . . T . . . Y.

Me: [laughing]. Oh. Faulty.

Mom: Brown ones or bad ones. You know? Then they'd go on and make peanut butter crackers out of them. I worked in lots of factories. A venetian blind factory. Another one where we took patches of fabric and glued them onto pages next to pictures of men in suits. I wish I could remember all of the factories I worked in.

> "I WAS PRETTY GOOD AT THE CAMOUFLAGE FACTORY TYING BITS OF MATERIALS"

15 Minutes with Mom

On Six Weeks with Ricky, Jelly Beans, and Kaka

Me: Didn't you go to Florida a few times?
Mom: Oh. Yes. That's right. Eddie took me once and Linda, too. And then I went down there with Linda and Brenda to your college graduations. And then I stayed down there for six weeks with you. Oooo. That was such a time.
Me: What do you mean?
Mom: I really loved being with you. We'd walk around the lake and feed the ducks. You took me to that place near Mexico.

15 Minutes with Mom

Me: Huh? Oh, the Everglades near the Gulf of Mexico.

Mom: But that ex-wife of yours. I spilled water in the refrigerator and went to mop it up with a dish towel and she snatched it out of my hands and flung it onto the counter saying, "You don't use my dish towels to wipe up spills." Then another time, remember you let me sleep in the bed and you and Jessica slept on the blow up bed? Well I went to paint my nails and she took the polish out of my hand and said I couldn't paint my nails while in her bed just like I was a child. Then you and me were downstairs and I was saying what a hard person she was when she called down saying, "I can hear you I know you're talking about me." And you called up,

"We're just talking about how nice you are."
[We both laugh].

Me: I'm sorry about that. I didn't know she'd done that to you.

Mom: I was happy to see Sunday come and sad to see Friday.

Me: Oh, when she left to fly to work and then came back.

Mom: Yeah.

Me: Well, I know now that some of it was me and not all her. It was tough. Didn't you work at a candy factory?

Mom: ooo eee. On Frederick Road. Fred Foose Candy. I don't think they exist anymore. That man chewed tobacco and would spit right on the floor. We made different colored jelly beans. I still can't eat jelly beans. [she laughs]. If I could remember there were a lot of places. I worked at the Solo Cup Company. I was working with the little cups for like medicine at hospitals. I'd have to take a sleeve and fill it up then put it in a case behind me then do it again. I was on night shift. I lost seven pounds in two weeks. [she laughs]. When that machine jammed the man would come and fix it in a snap. At another job I'd leave covered in flour.

Me: Was it the same bakery you talked about before?

Mom: Maybe. I'm not sure.

Me: Why did you leave and go to another factory?

Mom: I was trying to earn more money I started at .75 cents but never made more than $1.25. I was trying to improve myself. I made enough to keep a roof over our heads and food on the table and some clothes. One time Bobby said he'd pay the gas and electric bill. He went to pay it, then next I know I get a bill saying they'd shut off the power if we didn't pay. He'd bought a bat, ball, and glove and hid them in the shed out back. He said over and over, "I'm sorry." I told him he'd make us stay in the dark and we wouldn't be able to cook.

<u>Me</u>: How old was he?

<u>Mom</u>: A teenager. Oh, no. He left by the time he was a teen. About 10 or so. When I went to talk -- that's where his bed was -- I went to smack at him and he fell back and cried that I'd broke his hand. His daddy called the police on me. When the policeman got there and saw Bobby wasn't hurt, the police said, "Your mother didn't give you enough of a licking." Your daddy got mad and headed off to South Carolina.

15 Minutes with Mom

I'd come home from work at 11:00 and had to get back up at 7:00. Mama was such a big help watching you kids. One time Bobby smeared kaka on the wall.

<u>Me</u>: What? How old was he?

<u>Mom</u>: Kaka. On the porch wall. He was 2 or so. He took it out of his diaper and smeared it on the wall.

<u>Me</u>: Oh, my.

"Your mother didn't give you enough of a licking"

15 Minutes with Mom

On Rain, Getting Sick, and Pipe Smoking

Me: The rain is supposed to come hard tomorrow.

Mom: Well you bundle up and stay dry so you don't get sick.

Me: Mom -- you don't get sick from getting rained on.

Mom: Don't tell me. I'm 88 and I know you can get sick from getting wet. You can catch a chill and get sick.

Me: Well, why don't we get sick from taking a bath or going swimming?

Mom: Because you dry off right away. And the pool you're out in the warm sun. But on chilly days you can catch a chill. So put that in your pipe and smoke it. [we both laugh]

"SO PUT THAT IN YOUR PIPE AND SMOKE IT"

On Steak, Honey Bee, and Friendly's

Mom: Eddie is picking me up around five. Dinner is at 6:00.

Me: Where are you going?

Mom: I don't remember. He asked me if I like beef stew. I'm not that fond of beef anymore. I can have a steak every now and then. He said they have lots of pasta dishes, too.

Me: Well, be sure to know its name when you get home so I'll know. What's the first restaurant you ever went to?

Mom: We didn't go to restaurants when we lived down on the farm. We didn't have the money. First time I went to a restaurant would have been up here. We came up here in '49 -- the year Linda was born. I don't remember. When we went back at a place on Main Street [Bennettsville]. I think I like their beef stew. It was a family restaurant, but I don't recall the name of the place. I'd go to places to eat with Mary Lee and Lawrence.

Me: I remember a little place on the corner not far from Uncle Lawrence's place across from that super market on Ritchie Highway. It was an Italian place. Do you remember?

Mom: No. Not really. I used to like going to Honey Bee. Used to be when Irene and I were doing ceramics at the senior center we'd go there after. Sometimes Ann would meet us there when she was watching after this old lady. We used to go to Friendly's, too, till Ann got into it with Tracy [who works there] and Tracy told Ann not to come back. She has always been one to find fault with people. There was this doctor of hers in Glen Burnie I used to take her to. I had to go because she was out there talking crazy and the doctor needed me to help. Later, Mercy Hospital opened up over there on Quarterfield Road and he had a commercial, Dr. Kim. She said she'd like to put him in a coffin and drill holes in it and put him in it till he dies. She's out there.

Me: Why?

Mom: She hated him. She's been like that her whole life. She does crazy things.

Me: It's bipolar, too.

Mom: Yes, she is. Doctor says so. But I love her. She's been good to us -- to me. Helped us many times. I'm thankful for

15 Minutes with Mom

what she and Eddie Elmore did for us.
Well, I used to like going to McDonald's. I haven't been there in a while.

<u>Me</u>:   I guess people bring it all to you now.

<u>Mom</u>: That's right.

"I USED TO LIKE GOING TO McDONALD'S"

Made in the USA
Middletown, DE
08 May 2023